Katrine Hütterer & Yvonne Kalb

Simply Manifesting

Katrine Hütterer
& Yvonne Kalb

SIMPLY MANIFESTING

The Law of Assumption Easily Explained

Should this publication contain links to third-party websites, we do not accept any liability for their contents, as we do not adopt them as our own, but merely refer to their status at the time of initial publication.

This book is also available as e-book.

c/o skriptspektor e. U.
Robert-Preußler-Straße 13 / TOP 1
AT - 5020 Salzburg

Production and publishing: Independently published
Cover design: Yvonne Kalb
Cover design and image: Canva
ISBN: 9798476407959

First published in German under the title: „Einfach Manifestieren - Das Gesetz der Annahme leicht erklärt"
in March 2020.
Translation of the German edition by Katrine Hütterer.

www.team-huetterer.com

"An awakened imagination works with a purpose. It creates and conserves the desirable and transforms or destroys the undesirable."

Neville Goddard

CONTENTS

INTRODUCTION

Introduction

Hello and welcome to our book "Simply Manifesting". If you already know us, Katy & Yvonne aka Team Huetterer, a little bit, you know that this is our motto. Manifesting must be simple and easy!

When we first learned about the Law of Assumption (LOA),[1] it was anything but easy for us. There was very little information about it in our mother tongue German (Katy is Austrian, Yvonne is from Germany) and even that was uncoordinated, confusing, and often seemed complicated.

---

[1] LOA: What we believe about ourselves, and the world determines what experiences we have in life and what opportunities are open to us.

We studied the books and lectures of Neville Goddard[2] and Joseph Murphy[3] and finally came across the best-known LOA coaches of our time with whom we attended several courses and coaching sessions.

What we always lacked was a compact guide, an explanation of how we can best use the Law of Assumption for ourselves. What is the best method for me? When should I use it? How often? Lullaby or scene technique? Congratulatory scene or telephone technique? What is my "ending"? How am I supposed to know what the fulfilled wish feels like?

---

[2] Neville Lancelot Goddard was born in 1905 in St. Michael, Barbados. At the age of 17, he came to New York, where he first studied dance and acting. With his mentor Abdullah, he learned Hebrew for five years, studied the Kabbalah and esoteric Christianity. In the early fifties of the twentieth century, he settled in Los Angeles. For years, Neville taught techniques on how man can create his reality by using his imagination. He died in 1972.

[3] Dr Joseph Murphy was born in Ireland in 1898 into a Catholic family. After emigrating to the USA in 1922, he studied religious studies, philosophy, and law. From the 1940s he worked for magazines, radio and television stations and published numerous books. He published his major work at the age of 64. Murphy died in California in 1981.

Questions upon questions that had initially distracted us from our success with the LOA.

For this reason, you now have our answers to all these questions in this little book. In your hands is a summary of the most important aspects of using LOA – explained in an easy and understandable way.

We wish you lots of fun and success with "Simply Manifesting"!

Katy & Yvonne

PS: Please, dear reader, have mercy. Katy translated this book into English herself. Perhaps the phrasing is not always perfect, but the message is the point: Use the Law of Assumption to create your perfect life – it's easy and it works!

THE LAW OF ASSUMPTION

The Law of Assumption

"Imagination is the only reality."
Neville Goddard

This is probably the most famous and important quote by Neville Goddard. Our imagination is the only reality. What does this mean? This phrase explains us that we are the only cause of the phenomena in our lives, because with the help of our imagination we can influence and control our reality and our external world ourselves. This simple but for many people difficult to accept statement is basically the whole secret of the Law of Assumption. Everything that shows up in our lives, we have previously created ourselves through our assumptions and our imagination. What appears in our outside world now, are mostly our assumptions from the past. This is difficult for many people to acknowledge at first. However, the beauty of this universal law, which always works whether we use it consciously or (like most people) unconsciously, is that conversely, we have absolute power over the phenomena in our lives.

We can decide at any time to intervene consciously and only create what we want to have and experience in our lives. In this book you will learn how to do this most easily.

Neville put it in his lecture "Imagination Fulfills Itself" this way: *"Believe that it is real. Believe that it is true and that it will happen. Imagination will not disappoint you if you dare to accept something and persist in your acceptance, because imagination will fulfil itself in what becomes your life."*[4]

Our life in the outside always expresses only our inner self-talk. What we think about ourselves, about relationships, about money, about health, about other people, and the world in general – or perhaps fear, but

---

[4] http://realneville.com/txt/imagination_fulfills_itself.htm, as of 20th of March 2020.

in any case, believe, assume, is also shown to us in our outer world.

Imagination is belief and vice versa. Most of what we believe about ourselves, and others has been suggested to us over many, many years – mostly unconsciously. We all know that critical voice in our head that makes us feel bad about ourselves or the world. These can be, for example, old beliefs from childhood or limiting assumptions of our society such as "You'll never achieve anything" or "You can't have it all". Sentences like "The world is not a safe place", "Money is the root of all evil" and many more are deeply embedded in us, usually without us being aware of it.

Make a long story short: We imagine and manifest twenty-four hours a day, even while we sleep. Think about it: What thoughts do you fall asleep with? Are you worrying? Are you still having an argument with someone in your imagination? Are you thinking about worries at work? About the children's bad marks at school? How does your self-talk during the day sound? Is it different from the one before you go to sleep?

With these thoughts and the associated feelings that they make us feel, we unconsciously create our reality all the time. Unfortunately, this usually does not correspond to what we would like to have and experience in our lives. Therefore, it should be clear by now: We must actively intervene and use the Law of Assumption in our favour, otherwise it will use us. For this reason, we must consciously change our self-talk and our assumptions in such a way that our ideal, our desired life, can be realised. We must educate, yes: re-educate, our beliefs and our imagination.

How do we achieve this best? With conscious autosuggestion[5] or self-persuasion, because it can – consistently applied – erase our old, unconscious beliefs and overwrite them with the new, desired

[5] Autosuggestion is the process by which a person trains their unconscious to believe in something.

ones. The French pharmacist and author Émile Coué,[6] who is considered the founder of modern conscious autosuggestion, had this to say: *"Conscious autosuggestion, done with confidence, faith and perseverance, realises itself automatically."*

Now learn more about the conscious application of the Law of Assumption in this book. What are the four most important steps in applying the LOA? What is the best way to proceed, and which important terms should you know and, above all, understand? What does "creating a secondary cause" mean? What is the relocation exercise exactly about? What methods and techniques did Neville Goddard suggest? What should I do if I have experienced something terrible? What does 70x7 mean? Why does imagining on behalf of others make sense? Let's find the answers to these questions ...

---

[6] Émile Coué was born in Troyes (France) in 1857. He was a pharmacist and author as well as the founder of modern conscious autosuggestion. Coué died in Nancy (France) in 1926.

THE FOUR MOST IMPORTANT STEPS

The Four Most Important Steps

1. Know exactly what you want. Become aware of your desire, your ideal state.
2. Create a simple and short imaginative experience (scene or sentence) that would imply that your wish is true. Something that would naturally follow the wish fulfilled.
3. Go into the state akin to sleep – meditation, silence, stillness.
4. Repeat this imagination constantly until it completely dominates your mind, until it feels true and real.

After the seed has been sown through conscious autosuggestion, it is of course important to not dig it up again through our doubts. Experts recommend at least thirty, but ideally sixty to seventy minutes of conscious autosuggestion per day.

With the Law of Assumption, one thing is very important, but also very difficult for most people to handle: The "how", the "who" and the "when" are not in our power and we cannot influence them. That means, how and when exactly our wish will be fulfilled and who will contribute in what way, we must not concern ourselves with that, that would dig up the seed again.

It is perfectly normal to have doubts from time to time. This happens to all of us when we consciously work with the Law of Assumption, especially when success does not come immediately. But if we remain consistent and apply the LOA as a philosophy of life, we will eventually be able to free ourselves from our doubts sooner or later.

No matter what our desire is and no matter how many people it will take to make it happen, they will all get in motion to make it happen and it will seem perfectly natural to you. Neville once said: *"Looking back, it happened so naturally that you say to yourself,*

'Well, it would have happened anyway', and you quickly recover from that wonderful experience."

THE ONLY CAUSE

The Only Cause

"You are the cause of all the phenomena of your life."

Neville Goddard

An important aspect of the Law of Assumption is that we are the only cause of all phenomena in our lives. Far too often we create a secondary cause: we blame other people or circumstances for our problems. "My marriage could be great, but my husband won't work on it", "I'd love to, but I'm not fit enough" or "My job would be great, but my boss is just unbearable" are just a few examples of how we like to look for the reasons for our problems on the outside instead of in our inner assumptions.

In "At Your Command", Neville wrote the following: *"Put not your trust in men for men but reflect the being that you are and can only bring to you or do unto you that which you have first done unto yourself.*

'No man taketh away my life, I lay it down myself.' I have the power to lay it down and the power to take it

up again.

No matter what happens to man in this world it is never an accident. It occurs under the guidance of an exact and changeless Law.

'No man' (manifestation) 'comes unto me except the father within me draw him,' and 'I and my father are one.' Believe this truth and you will be free. Man has always blamed others for that which he is and will continue to do so until he finds himself as cause of all. 'I AM' comes not to destroy but to fulfill. 'I AM,' the awareness within you, destroys nothing but ever fill full the molds or conception one has of one's self.

It is impossible for the poor man to find wealth in this world no matter how he is surrounded with it until he first claims himself to be wealthy. For signs follow, they do not precede. To constantly kick and complain against the limitations of poverty while remaining poor in consciousness is to play the fool's game. Changes cannot take place from that level of consciousness for life in constantly outpicturing all levels.

Follow the example of the prodigal son. Realize that you,

yourself brought about this condition of waste and lack and make the decision within yourself to rise to a higher level where the fatted calf, the ring, and the robe await your claim.

There was no condemnation of the prodigal when he had the courage to claim this inheritance as his own. Others will condemn us only as long as we continue in that for which we condemn ourselves. So: 'Happy is the man that condemneth himself not in that which he alloweth.' For to life nothing is condemned. All is expressed.

Life does not care whether you call yourself rich or poor; strong or weak. It will eternally reward you with that which you claim as true of yourself. The measurements of right and wrong belong to man alone. To life there is nothing right or wrong. As Paul stated in his letters to the Romans: 'I know and am persuaded by the Lord Jesus that there is nothing unclean of itself, but to him that esteemeth anything to be unclean, to him it is unclean.' Stop asking yourself whether you are worthy or unworthy to receive that which you desire. You, as man, did not create the desire. Your desires are ever fashioned within you because of what you now claim yourself to be. When a man is hungry, (without thinking) he automatically desires food. When imprisoned, he automatically desires freedom and so forth. Your desires contain within themselves the plan of self-expression. So leave all judgments out of the picture and rise in consciousness to the level of your desire and make yourself one with it by claiming it to be so now. For: 'My grace is sufficient for thee. My strength is made perfect in weakness.'

Have faith in this unseen claim until the conviction is born within you that it is so. Your confidence in this claim will pay great rewards. Just a little while and he, the thing desired, will come. But without faith it is impossible to realize anything. Through faith the worlds were framed because 'faith is the substance of the thing hoped for – the evidence of the thing not yet seen.'

Don't be anxious or concerned as to results. They will follow just as surely as day follows night. Look upon your desires – all of them – as the spoken words of God, and every word or desire a promise. The reason most of us fail to realize our desires is because we are constantly conditioning them. Do not condition your desire. Just accept it as it comes to you. Give thanks for it to the point that you are grateful for having already received it – then go about your way in peace.

Such acceptance of your desire is like dropping seed – fertile seed – into prepared soil. For when you can drop the thing desired in consciousness, confident that it shall appear, you have done all that is expected to you. But to be worried or concerned about the HOW of your desire maturing is to hold these fertile seeds in a mental grasp, and, therefore, never to have dropped them in the soil of confidence.

The reason men condition their desires is because they constantly judge after the appearance of being and see the things as real – forgetting that the only reality is the consciousness back of them. To see things as real is to deny that all things are possible to God. The man who is imprisoned and sees his four walls as real is automatically denying the urge or promise of God within him of freedom. A question often asked when this statement is made is; If one's desire is a gift of God, how can you say that if one desires to kill a man that such a desire is good and therefore God sent? In answer to this let me say that no man desires to kill another. What he does desire is to be freed from such a one. But because he does not believe that the desire to be free from such a one contains within itself the powers of freedom, he conditions that desire and sees the only way to express such freedom is to destroy the man – forgetting that the life wrapped within the desire has ways that he, as man, knows not of. Its ways are past finding out. Thus man distorts the gifts of God through his lack of faith.

Problems are the mountains spoken of that can be removed if one has but the faith of a grain of a mustard seed. Men approach their problem as did the old lady who, on attending service and hearing the priest say, 'If you had but the faith of a grain of a mustard seed you would say unto yonder mountain 'be thou removed' and it shall be removed, and nothing is impossible to you.'"[7]

By the way, Yvonne describes this topic very impressively in her extremely honest book "Hoppla, ich bin die einzige Ursache… für die Phänomene meines Lebens" (currently only available in German).[8] She describes how much she got bogged down by her negative assumptions, how much she repeatedly thought that other people, the circumstances of her life, and even fate were the reason for her problems, fears, and compulsions.

That is why our message to you is to make yourself aware over and over again: *You* are the only cause!

---

[7] http://nevillegoddardpdf.com/free-books-and-lectures/neville-goddard-free-pdf-at-your-command/, as of 13th of September 2021.
[8] Kalb, Yvonne: Hoppla, ich bin die einzige Ursache… für die Phänomene meines Lebens. Wie das Gesetz der Annahme mein Leben verändert hat, Independently published, ISBN: 9798620550623.

"To pray successfully you must have clearly defined objectives. You must know what you want before you can ask for it. You must know what you want before you can feel that you have it, and prayer is the feeling of the fulfilled desire."

Neville Goddard

THE FIRST PRINCIPLE

The First Principle "I AM"

Neville Goddard always recommended his students: "When in doubt, go back to the first principle." So, what is the first principle? It is called: I AM.[9]

When we really know who we are, we can just let the Law of Assumption happen. We can let our conscious autosuggestion happen. Because when we really know who we are, we are completely in trust.

Neville's first principle refers to Psalm 46:11 of the Bible *"Be still and know that I am God"*, to our I AM, our pure divine consciousness. When we experience I AM or I AM GOD, we leave our old self-image completely behind and experience ourselves as greater than all our wishes and dreams put together. This God-consciousness is an indescribably beautiful and powerful state which is always accessible to us.

---

[9] https://freeneville.com/the-first-principle-neville-goddard-pdf-june-1969/, as of 13th of September 2021.

Since it is easy for us to accept the self-image of fulfilled desire from this special I AM state, Neville recommended the first principle as help against any doubts or difficulties in applying the Law of Assumption. So, whenever you feel that you can no longer get into the state of your fulfilled desire or that you are doubting or digging up the seed again, go back to the first principle. You can use the following "I AM" meditation for this.

"I AM" MEDITATION

"I AM" Meditation

Neville told us in "Your Faith is your Fortune": *"The invitation of the scriptures, 'To be absent from the body and be present with the Lord' [Corinthians 5:8, Corinthians 5:3, Colossians 2:5], is not given to a select few; it is a sweeping call to all mankind. The body from which you are invited to escape is your present conception of yourself with all of its limitations, while the Lord with whom you are to be present is your awareness of being.*

To accomplish this seemingly impossible feat, you take your attention away from your problem and place it upon just being. You say silently but feelingly, 'I AM'. Do not condition this awareness but continue declaring quietly, 'I AM – I AM'. Simply feel that you are faceless and formless and continue doing so until you feel yourself floating.

'Floating' is a psychological state which completely denies the physical. Through practice in relaxation and willfully refusing to react to sensory impressions, it is possible

to develop a state of consciousness of pure receptivity. It is a surprisingly easy accomplishment. In this state of complete detachment, a definite singleness of purposeful thought can be indelibly engraved upon your unmodified consciousness. This state of consciousness is necessary for true meditation.

This wonderful experience of rising and floating is the signal that you are absent from the body or problem and are now present with the Lord; in this expanded state you are not conscious of being anything, but I AM – I AM; you are only conscious of being.

When this expansion of consciousness is attained, within this formless deep of yourself, give form to the new conception by claiming and feeling yourself to be that which you, before you entered into this state, desired to be. You will find that within this formless deep of yourself all things appear to be divinely possible. Anything that you sincerely feel yourself to be while in this expanded state becomes, in time, your natural expression."[10]

In a nutshell: Withdraw, go into silence, and repeat "I AM" over and over again. On your inhale you think "I" and on your exhale you think "AM". Repeat this until you feel calmer. Then you can go back into your usual routine of conscious autosuggestion.

Of course, you can also use the "I AM" meditation in everyday life if you don't feel like yourself or if you feel too overwhelmed by the outside world.

---

[10] https://www.yourfaithisyourfortune.com/tag/your-faith-is-your-fortune/page/2 and https://www.law-of-attraction-haven.com/support-files/your-faith-is-your-fortune-neville-goddard.pdf, as of 13th of September 2021.

THE RELOCATION EXERCISE

The Relocation Exercise

An excellent preliminary exercise for using conscious autosuggestion and exploring your desired state is the relocation exercise. Neville learned this exercise from his teacher Abdullah and has always recommended it to his students:

"My old friend Abdullah gave me this exercise. Every day I would sit in my living room where I could not use the phone. With my eyes closed, I assumed I was sitting on the chair next to the phone in the hallway. Then I felt I was back in the living room. I did this again and again as I discovered the feeling of the changing movement. This exercise was very helpful for me. If you try it, you will find that you become very loose when you do the exercise. Practice the art of movement."[11]

Neville mentioned again and again in his lectures that he practised the relocation exercise every day. Why? Well, no exercise reveals our true being to us

---

[11] https://www.kraftdeswollens.de/imaginativer-umzug-neville-goddard-zitate/, as of 13th of September 2021.

humans so intensely. We move away from the physical to the spiritual. The relocation exercise is the art of mental movement. It teaches us to think *from* our desire and not just think *of* our desire. The mind goes first, the body follows. This is the basis of the Law of Assumption.

We keep believing that the world we perceive with our senses is reality, but do not realise that this reality is also only an imagination. Even our sensory perceptions do not come from our mind or arise through our senses but are imagined by us. Test it yourself: Close your eyes, imagine a rose, and breathe in its fragrance. You have only imagined it and yet you have perceived the scent of the rose. You can also imagine slicing a lemon and biting into one of the slices. Do you feel on your lip and taste on your tongue how sour the lemon is?

As long as we are identified with our body, we are convinced that we are only human, and that imagination is one of our faculties - but not that we *are* pure imagination. If we practise the relocation exercise, the art of mental movement, regularly, we realise that we are immortal beings in a mortal body and can travel to any place of our choice at any time.

Here is a guide to practise the relocation exercise:

First you sit in your living room and while sitting there you then imagine that you are in your bathroom. The moment you imagine that you are in the bathroom, you have already imaginatively moved into your bathroom. Now you can perceive your world from there and ask yourself:

- What do you see, feel, smell, and hear?

- What is in front of you, next to you and behind you?

- Where is the living room, the kitchen, the bedroom now?

- Where is your coffee machine? Your toothbrush? Your mobile phone? Your alarm clock?

Gradually you will forget that you are in the living room and have the feeling that you are in the bathroom. Then change the room and go into the kitchen. Notice everything there, too. Where is the bathroom now? The bedroom? What do you see? What can you touch?

Then go into the next room, then to the next supermarket, then to your workplace. Keep playing and practising.

You will soon notice that the more often you change the room, the more your mind relaxes and the more swiftly you move in spirit. The relocation exercise is the best exercise to train your imagination without any pressure, because it is not about manifesting and wish fulfilment, but only about the exercise of thinking *from* the state instead of thinking *about* the state.

"It is not what you want that you attract; you attract what you believe to be true. Therefore, get into the spirit of these mental conversations and give them the same degree of reality that you would a telephone conversation."

Neville Goddard

BUYING THE PEARL

Buying the Pearl

If you have already studied the Law of Assumption, you may have heard the expression "to buy the pearl" and wondered what it means. Learn now what Neville was talking about. "The Pearl of Great Price" is one of his most famous lectures. The most important section for us reads: *"If you think for a moment that you can hold on to a little thing, if that doesn't work, you can't buy the pearl. So, when I buy the pearl, I go all out and live by it. And there is nothing else in this world, only this pearl, and I live by it. That pearl is your own wonderful human imagination."*[12]

By "buying the pearl" is meant going "all in", internalising and living the Law of Assumption. Day and night. Everything else that would only be a secondary cause, such as laying cards, going to an

---

12 https://www.kraftdeswollens.de/die-perle-neville-goddard-zitate/, as of 13th of September 2021.

astrologer, believing that we would only get ahead with the help of a certain person or a certain thing, we must let go of all that. There is nothing but the Law of Assumption and our imagination. There is nothing except us. There is no secondary cause.

But let us tell you: We all sell the pearl repeatedly. It just happens. Even Neville has admitted to still selling the pearl unintentionally after decades of using LOA.

All that matters is that we get ourselves back on track.

70 x 7 = PERSISTENCE

70 x 7 = Persistence

Perhaps you have also asked yourself what 70x7 is all about? Neville kept mentioning these numbers - but what was he trying to tell us?

This is derived from the Bible: Peter asked Jesus how often he should forgive. Jesus answered Peter that he should forgive seventy times seven (Matthew 18:22). Seven is the number of perfection (see for example the completion of creation after seven days in Genesis). The number seventy speaks of the attainment of perfection (e.g., Psalm 90:10 or Daniel 9:24).[13]

For us, this does not mean that we should now repeat our imaginative action or our conscious autosuggestion exactly 490 times. No, this is more about symbolism, and this stands for persistence,

---

[13] https://www.bibelstudium.de/articles/4241/490-mal-vergeben.html, as of 20th of March 2020.

namely persistence in the application of the Law of Assumption.

We have heard from many of our coachees that staying persistent is their biggest challenge in LOA. We have therefore developed our online courses, in which we stay connected with our participants if they wish to do so. We support them with advice and action (in German language only).

How much easier is it to say, "It's not working!" instead of staying persistent? Perhaps we end our conscious autosuggestion too soon because we "can't get into it" or we miss opportunities during the day to imagine or to return to the desired state when we realise that we had fallen out.

Only when a state has its naturalness and has become a fixed part of our self-perception, it will show and manifest in our outer world in the way we have desired. Sometimes it only takes one short imagination, sometimes it takes many sessions of conscious autosuggestion and lots of self-conviction.

Even Neville could not predict how long it would take for a wish to come true and manifest on the outside, but he advised us to be consistent: 70 x 7. Go "all in". Be persistent.

"With this belief firmly established decide what would be a relative, rational interval of time in which such a desire could be realized. Again, let me remind you not to shorten the interval of time because you are anxious to receive your desire; make it a natural interval. No one can give you the time interval.

Only you can say what

the natural interval would

be to you. The interval of

time is relative, that is, no

two individuals would

give the same

measurement of time for

the realization of their

desire. "

Neville Goddard

STATE AKIN TO SLEEP

State Akin to Sleep

For successful conscious autosuggestion it is essential to "switch off" our will and we achieve this through the state that Neville called "state akin to sleep". It is an important tool, without mastering the state akin to sleep we cannot correctly apply the Law of Assumption. We know this sleep-like state, which is natural for us humans, from the moments just before falling asleep or just after waking up, when we are between waking and sleeping. We experience something similar when we lose ourselves in a daydream.

From our everyday life, we are used to regulating things with our will. But knowing the LOA, now we understand that with our willpower we only strengthen the situation we are currently in. However, since we want to consciously change our situation, we must go into the state akin to sleep before we can start with conscious autosuggestion or prayer, as Neville Goddard and Joseph Murphy called it. We are in this state when we feel tired and exhausted, but also – as already mentioned – in the evening before going to sleep and in the morning after waking up. Therefore, it is also ideal to use these times for conscious autosuggestion.

But we can also create this state consciously, for this purpose we withdraw to a quiet place and go into silence. We sit or lie down comfortably and make sure that we remain undisturbed for the next while. Then we concentrate on our breath. If thoughts still arise, we let them pass by like clouds in the sky.

We continue to focus on our breath until we feel the body and mind becoming more and more still. Many beginners find it difficult to get into the state akin to sleep and/or relaxation at the beginning. This is normal and no reason to worry. If this is the case for you, then stay consistent, because practice makes perfect.

THE SCENE TECHNIQUE

The Scene Technique (Visualisation)

The scene technique is probably the technique most often mentioned by Neville Goddard. In the state akin to sleep, we imagine a scene that presupposes the fulfilment of our wish. A scene that we would, even *would have to*, experience after the fulfilment of our desire. To use Neville's words, *"The end is where we begin."* So first we must be clear about what exactly we want, what we really desire. We need to explore the state we want to achieve (such as being happy, being free, etc.). So, we must ask ourselves: *What do I really want?*

Then we create a scene that would naturally follow the fulfilment of our wish. Neville favoured the so-called congratulatory scene: In our imagination a person we know congratulates us on the fulfilment of our wish. This scene should never last longer than a few seconds and can include a hug, a handshake, or the clinking of champagne glasses during a toast – in short: something that "seals" our success.

Another possibility would be the telephone scene, which Neville also liked to use very much – especially when he imagined on behalf of others. He would simply imagine the person calling him and telling him about their success (wish fulfilled). Of course, this also works in the other direction: We imagine telling a friend or relative about our fulfilled desire on the phone.

Important: We always see the scene from our own eyes – we do not look at it as a third party from the outside. We can ask ourselves the following questions to work out our scene:

- What would I experience?

- What would have my special attention?

- What do I like about what I see, hear, smell, taste, feel or think?

- What would be different in contrast to how I feel right now?

(... if my wish had already been fulfilled.)

Once we have created a (short!) scene, we enter the state akin to sleep and let it play repeatedly. If we drift off, we gently bring ourselves back to our scene.

"All things express their nature. As you wear a feeling, it becomes your nature. It might take a moment or a year – it is entirely dependent upon the degree of conviction. As doubts vanish and you can feel "I AM this", you begin to develop the fruit or the nature of the thing you are feeling yourself to be."

Neville Goddard

THE LULLABY METHOD

The Lullaby Method

The lullaby method does not work much differently from the scene technique, but instead of the scene we use a sentence that implies that our wish has already been fulfilled. As early as 1910, the psychotherapist Charles Baudouin[14] taught the effectiveness of a sentence as a lullaby: *"The simplest and most effective way to suggest the desired idea to the subconscious is to condense it into a short, memorable phrase, which is then constantly repeated - as if it were a lullaby."*

Our sentence should contain that we have already achieved our goal. What would we say to ourselves when our wish has been fulfilled? Neville usually used a simple "Thank you, Father!", we can of course use any other phrase that suits us. "I did it!", "That's

---

[14] Charles Baudouin was born on 26th of July 1893 in Nancy, France. He was a French-Swiss psychoanalyst and writer. Baudouin died on 25th of August 1963 in Saconnex-d'Arve, Geneva (Switzerland).

great!", "Bingo!", "That's wonderful!" or "Yeah!" would be a few examples.

In practice, we now apply the sentence in the same way as the scene: In the state akin to sleep, we repeat our phrase over and over again, completely monotonously.

It is important to not let the mind take over during conscious autosuggestion with the lullaby method and to think about what the sentence all entails. We have thought about and defined this in detail beforehand (when asking the question "What do I really want?").

Remember: If you know it, your unconscious also knows it.

A mistake of many users is to make the sentence a secondary cause. Your personal phrase fits as it is. Don't worry too much about the sentence. We could just say a single letter to ourselves, as long as we associate it with our fulfilled wish even this would work.

If we digress from our sentence in the state akin to sleep, we gently guide ourselves back to it. If images arise, we allow them, but we do not hold on to them or lose ourselves in concentrating on them. If they want to go, we let them go. We stay steady with our phrase. If problems with concentration arise, it can be helpful to speak the sentence half aloud.

THE FISHING METHOD

The Fishing Method

The Fishing Method is all about feeling and exploring the desired state. The great advantage of this method is, that it can be used at any time – during everyday life as well as in deep meditation. Mental movement is also important for the Fishing Method. We pull the "sometime" into the "now" and the "somewhere" into the "here". So, with the Fishing Method, we pull the feeling of our wish already fulfilled into the here and now.

We start, as with the other methods, by getting clear:

- What do I want? (What is the end?)

- What would be (at least) the three most beautiful things if it were already true?

- What would be (at least) three not so beautiful things if it were already true?

Important: The more precisely we have defined the final state, the easier it is to immerse ourselves into this state and perceive it as real. The exploration of a state allows us to already experience this state - this makes it much easier for us to imagine.

As soon as the answers to the questions above are clear, we can start with the Fishing Method. We ask ourselves the question: "How would I feel in this moment, when I realised that I had actually done it? ______, exactly as I had imagined it at the time?"

We can now also imagine a scene in which we would naturally think of having made it. The scene is only a tool to help us, not a secondary cause. We can now have an inner self-talk from the state of the already fulfilled wish, such as:

"I have actually made it. I am (or have) reached ______, just as I had imagined at the time. That's just great!"

How would we talk to ourselves once the wish is fulfilled? What would we say to ourselves at that moment?

Neville said once: "*Ask yourself this question: How would I feel if I were already ____? The moment you ask this question SERIOUSLY, the answer will come. No human being can tell another the satisfaction of his desire. It is up to each person to experience the feeling and the joy of this automatic change of consciousness. The feeling one encounters in response to self-inquiry is the foundation stone on which conscious change is built. All things express their nature. If you carry a feeling constantly, it becomes your nature. Your only task is to keep your attention on the state of the desire already fulfilled with minimum effort.*"[15]

Mr. Twenty Twenty, one of the best-known English-speaking LOA teachers, with whom Katy had a wonderful conversation, which you can read in her

---

[15] Neville Goddard, source unknown.

book “Geschafft! Erfolgreich durch Manifestation” (currently only available in German), invented the “Coffee Game”, which also exists in the variants “Peanut Butter Method” or “Petrol Method”.

In keeping with Neville, he recommends not simply imagining that you have reached your goal, but rather *feeling* how it would feel to drink your coffee (buy peanut butter, pay for petrol at the petrol station) and have already achieved what you wished for.

We can, of course, extend this game to anything we do regularly or that may not feel so good now because our goal has not yet been achieved. The important thing here is to explore the state of fulfilled desire.

When we have really defined what we want, explored the state, and applied the Fishing Method in the state akin to sleep, it is easy for us to return to this state even during our daily life. We surrender to this feeling of gratitude and relief at the wish fulfilled. “Wonderful!”

"You do not need to work out anything. The works are finished. The principle by which all things are made and without which there is not anything made that is made is eternal. You are this principle. Your awareness of being is this everlasting law."

Neville Goddard

REMEMBER WHEN?

Remember When?

When using the Remember When Method (in the German-speaking LOA community we use the terms "I remember, when ..." or "Do you remember ...?") we contrast two contrary assumptions or states. We place the current state of consciousness in the past (by saying that we still remember it) and speak of the desired state of consciousness as if it were now. So, we move the present state into the past and thus pull the state of our ideal into the present. The formula for this is: "I remember it as ________ but now _______ and I feel _______!"

Neville said in a lecture on the Remember When method: *"This principle can be used in a destructive or constructive way. You can say: 'I remember when this was a glorious building and look at it no' as you become aware of rubble where once a glorious building stood. Or you can stand on rubble and say: 'I remember when this was all rubble', as you imagine a glorious building. You can say: 'I remember when my friend had nothing and now he has much', or: 'I remember when he had much and now he is so poor.' You can say: 'I remember when she was healthy', which could imply she is now ill, or 'I remember when they were unknown', implying they are now famous. So, you see what power was in that revelation. It's entirely up to you how you use your imagination, but the operation of your creative power is completely up to you. You make the decision and are therefore responsible for its effect on the world."*[16]

In the beginning, we take a little more time with the Remember When method and talk ourselves deeper and deeper into the new self-image. We do this until we feel relieved, grateful, and satisfied. This method is simple, always applicable and we immediately shift our attention from the undesired state to the desired one.

---

16 https://freeneville.com/free-neville-goddard-lecture-i-remember-when-1968/, as of 13th of September 2021.

REVISION

Revision

Revision is a follow-up method of the Law of Assumption. To work with this method, we must already know what we want. With the LOA, if we don't like our reality, we can simply say to ourselves "I don't accept it!" Of course, this also applies to our past.

In revision, events that have already happened are rewritten in retrospect. In revising, we divert our attention from an event we disliked to a new, different direction.

Any stressful events from the past that come up in the memory can also be re-written with the help of revision. So, if you are not the person you want to be today and if your present memories have made you the person you are today, then other memories would clearly make you a different person. By re-writing, you can shape your memories to create the person you choose to be.

Neville Goddard's variant of revising the entire day in retrospect is also very popular, i.e., rewinding the day in the mind's eye when going to bed in the evening – but this time with exclusively positive experiences. So, every bad day becomes a good day, and every good day becomes a great day. In the process, we feel a great sense of relief. We can ask ourselves the question: "How would I feel if the day had been a complete success and full of beautiful moments?"

This also works in the other direction, then we call it prevision. In this case, before getting up in the morning, we imagine that it is already evening and that our day has been a complete success and full of wonderful surprises. Here, too, we perceive the feeling of relief.

Neville explained the "Pruning Shears of Revision" in his 1954 lecture of the same name as follows: *"Now this is how we do it. At the end of my day, I review the day; I don't judge it, I simply review it. I look over the entire day, all the episodes, all the events, all the conversations, all the meetings, and then as I see it clearly in my mind's eye,*

I rewrite it. I rewrite it and make it conform to the ideal day I wish I had experienced. I take scene after scene and rewrite it, revise it, and having revised my day, then in my imagination I relive that day, the revised day, and I do it over and over in my imagination until this seeming imagined state begins to take on to me the tones of reality. It seems that it's real, that I actually did experience it and I have found from experience that these revised days, if really lived, will change my tomorrows. When I meet people tomorrow that today disappointed me, they will not tomorrow, for in me I have changed the very nature of that being, and having changed him, he bears witness tomorrow of the change that took place within me. It is my duty to take this garden and really make it a garden by daily using the pruning shears of revision."[17]

The important thing to remember is that revision is more about *how we feel* than about the actual situation

---

17 https://archive.org/stream/NevilleGoddard003/the_pruning_shears_of_revision_djvu.txt, as of 13th of September 2021.

we are experiencing. Revision is one of the most powerful tools to create the life you really want.

IMAGINING ON BHEALF OF ANOTHER

Imagining on Behalf of Another

A wonderful way to live the Law of Assumption is to lovingly imagine on behalf of another. Neville (and many others) called this the "Golden Rule".[18] He said in "Prayer, The Art Of Believing": *"To awaken a state within another it must first be awake within you. The state you would transmit to another can only be transmitted if it is believed by you. Therefore, to give is to receive. You cannot give what you do not have, and you have only what you believe. So, to believe a state as true of another not only awakens that state within the other but it makes it alive within you. You are what you believe."*[19]

By the way, for many people it is easier to first imagine others happy and fulfilled before they can do that for themselves. The good thing is: By awakening

---

[18] The Golden Rule is the principle of treating others as one wants to be treated.

[19] http://nevillegoddardpdf.com/free-books-and-lectures/prayer-the-art-of-believing-free-neville-goddard download/, as of 13th of September 2021.

the state of happiness in the imagination for "another" person, they also awaken it in themselves. For separation is only illusion and there is only one consciousness. What we see in others we also see in ourselves because we are one with them. Thus, lovingly imagining on behalf of others is also always helpful for ourselves.

Another aspect when imagining lovingly for other people is important: "conversion". Many LOA followers want the best for friends and family and try to convert them to the Law. But our task is not to proselytise others, but first to lovingly imagine on behalf of them. Often these people then come of their own accord and want to know more about it. Telling a person about the Law of Assumption and wanting to convert him or her also means that we keep this person in his or her undesirable state. We keep him or her small. Change can only happen inside, through our imagination and because there is only one consciousness, one "I AM", we can also reach the other person on this level. Do not skip imagining lovingly on behalf of another! You are imagining, as already mentioned, not only for them, but always for yourself as well. Neville, too, only imagined lovingly on behalf of other people.

“Use your imagination lovingly on behalf of another.“

Neville Goddard

WHAT CAN I DO?

What Can I Do?

The following quote from Neville, on which many users of the Law of Assumption like to "rest", is often misunderstood: *"The question is often asked, 'What should be done between the assumption of the wish fulfilled and its realization?'*

Nothing. It is a delusion that, other than assuming the feeling of the wish fulfilled, you can do anything to aid the realization of your desire.

You think that you can do something, you want to do something; but actually, you can do nothing. The illusion of the free will to do is but ignorance of the Law of Assumption upon which all action is based.

Everything happens automatically.

All that befalls you, all that is done by you – happens.

Your assumptions, conscious or unconscious, direct all thought and action to their fulfillment.

To understand the Law of Assumption, to be convinced of its truth, means getting rid of all the illusions about free will to act. Free will actually means freedom to select any idea you desire.

By assuming the idea already to be a fact, it is converted into reality. Beyond that, free will ends, and everything happens in harmony with the concept assumed."[20]

What Neville is telling us is, that we don't have to do anything *willingly* after we have used conscious autosuggestion and entered the state of fulfilled desire. He is not telling you to lie down on the couch and wait for your wish to come true. He says you don't have to do anything *out of your will*. You don't have to think hard about *how* to achieve the fulfilment of your wish, because everything will arrange itself. You may get an impulse to do this or that. Then do it. It will lead you one step further towards the fulfilment of your desire. In the end, everything falls into place and will feel natural. It couldn't have come any other way.

---

[20] https://www.thepowerofawareness.org/chapter-twenty-one, as of 13th of September 2021.

And please don't forget: the most important thing about imagining and manifesting is having fun. Play with your desires!

Have fun with it!

CONCLUSION

Conclusion

We are very pleased that this book has found its way to you. Whether you start with the Law of Assumption right now or later, one thing is clear to us: The knowledge about LOA will never let you go. We also know that the more people lovingly use and apply the LOA for themselves and their environment, the more our world will change for the better. So, what could be more wonderful than that?

There is only one thing we would like to say to you: Remain persistent! Fulfil your only task, put yourself daily for at least thirty to seventy minutes into the state akin to sleep and experience there with all your senses the state of your wish fulfilled. When you know this state of consciousness as well as a second skin (through the consistency with the conscious autosuggestion), then feel into it again and again in your daily life (fishing method). Live from the state of your wish fulfilled!

There will possibly be ups and downs. We can tell you a thing or two about it, believe us. Yvonne has written very openly in her books not only about her personal story with fears and compulsions, but also about her doubts and difficulties in applying the Law of Assumption.

In LOA circles we call this the "what-the-hell effect" (WTH), when suddenly the exact opposite of our aspired ideal appears in our life. But this is also completely normal: On the one hand, it may be that you are still exerting too much willpower because your wish is sooooo important to you. In this case, go back to the first principle and become aware of your divine I AM again. On the other hand, it is simply the case that our assumptions usually show up with a time delay in our supposed reality. What we experience in the here and now are actually our assumptions and our beliefs from the past. So please, don't stress and start doubting if the WTH effect happens. Also remember, Neville called our path to manifesting our desires the "bridge of incidents", so if you are not yet where you want to be, be aware: You are on the bridge of incidents and not at "the end" yet.

In Katy's book "Geschafft! Erfolgreich durch Manifestieren" (currently only available in German) you can read many very different success stories of users of the Law, which are very motivating and inspiring. Especially in times of uncertainty and doubt, such stories do us a lot of good.

And please, always be aware

of your divine consciousness.

Your YOU ARE.

Your I AM.

We all are.

ONE.

Let us close this book with the words of Neville Goddard:

"The game of life is won by those who compare their thoughts and feelings within to what appears on the outside. And the game is lost by those who do not recognize this law. Being consumed by anger, they see no change in their world.

But if they would change their mood, their circumstances would change. Then they would recognize the law behind their world."[21]

Have fun imagining and manifesting with the Law of Assumption!

[21] https://freeneville.com/the-game-of-life-neville-goddard-pdf/, as of 13th of September 2021.

Dear reader!

If you enjoyed this book and it inspired you to finally create the life of your dreams, we would be very happy to receive a positive review.

Thank you!

MORE BOOKS

Hütterer, Katrine/Fischer, Norman P.: Imagine and Grow Rich. Create the Life of Your Dreams, Indpendently published, ISBN: 9798481115269.

Hütterer, Katrine/Kalb, Yvonne: Create the Life You Want. Manifestation Journal, Independently published, ISBN: 979-8479560033.

Hütterer, Katrine/Kalb, Yvonne: Life Is Beautiful. Gratitude Journal, Independently published, ISBN: 979-8480989168.

Hütterer Katrine/Kalb, Yvonne: Manifest Your Dream Life. Write Your Own Future, Independently published, ISBN: 979-8479092619.

KATRINE HÜTTERER

Katrine Hütterer

Katrine Hütterer, M. A., studied journalism and communication science and worked as a journalist for many years. In her mid-thirties, she experienced a burnout because, as a perfectionist, she constantly put herself under pressure and overtaxed herself.

Many coachings and trainings in the field of life support and (mental) coaching as well as a professional reorientation were the result.

Today she is an author, editor, and mentor. Together with Yvonne Kalb, she forms Team Huetterer. They both love and live gratitude practice and the art of manifesting with the Law of Assumption (LOA) according to Neville Goddard.

After some years as an expat in Belgium, she now lives with her husband, kids, and cat in Austria.

YVONNE KALB

Yvonne Kalb

Yvonne Kalb is a state-certified educator and trained specialist for early education and has worked as an educator for many years.

She – and her family – suffered a lot from her fears and compulsions, which made a normal life almost impossible for her. Yvonne was finally able to get a grip on these with the help of coaching and personal development. Many trainings and further education in these areas and a professional reorientation were the result.

Living gratitude practice and the constant application of the Law of Assumption (LOA) according to Neville Goddard have also improved her quality of life immensely. Today, she describes the LOA as the key to her final liberation from her "prison" caused by her illness. She tells her story in her book „Hoppla, ich bin die einzige Ursache … für die Phänomene meines Lebens“.

She now is a certified coach, author, gratitude & manifestation trainer and together with Katrine Hütterer forms Team Huetterer.

Yvonne lives in Germany with her husband, son and cat.

The authors do not assume any liability for the topicality, correctness, completeness, or quality of the information provided. Liability claims against the authors relating to material or non-material damage caused by the use or non-use of the information provided or using incorrect or incomplete information are excluded in principle, unless it can be proven that the authors acted with intent or gross negligence.

First publication in English language:

September 2021

www.team-huetterer.com
www.katrinehuetterer.com
www.yvonnekalb.com

Printed in Great Britain
by Amazon